T0343810

Washing My Mother's Body

Washing My Mother's Body

A Ceremony for Grief

JOY HARJO

Art by DANA TIGER

Introduction

I never know what a poem, song, or other composition will offer. This poem surprised me. I was in the middle of writing a poetry collection involving research and interrogation of family history, particularly the removal of my father's family from our homelands in the southeastern United States, when the first lines of "Washing My Mother's Body" tumbled out onto the page: "I never got to wash my mother's body when she died./I return to take care of her in memory./That's how I make peace when things are left undone." I had to run to keep up with the poem as it unfolded from the emotional depths of grief that I didn't know I was still carrying.

Grief is uncontainable. It is a shapeshifter. One day, it is a few quiet tears. The next, a deluge and you tread through the salty waters for hours. As I wrote, I did not know what I would find. The poem was showing me as I followed it. Death is the companion of life. It remains a mystery. We will all eventually leave on a journey for which there is no discernable earth map. Poetry is a tool for the investigation of mystery, for finding words when there are no words. Words sung or spoken are often the doorways that begin and end the ceremony of transformative moments of our lives.

I wanted to honor my mother's life by washing her body when she died. I wasn't allowed that opportunity. She felt torn from me, a ritual undone. I was the oldest child, the oldest daughter, and I knew her in a way that no one else knew her. Maybe that is true of every child in every family. We each know our mother in a manner that is unlike any other. The mother root is the deepest root in each of us. This poem taught me that in poetry, you can bend time to go back and take care of what needs to be done.

If anyone knows about grief, it is the artist visionary Dana Tiger. She and her family have endured more than their share of loss. If anyone knows about joy, it is also Dana Tiger. For a lifetime, she has uplifted our community with brilliant images that tell the mythic and ordinary stories of our lives. Tiger's art honors our Mvskoke community, reminds us that we have a special place in the earth story. Both Tiger and I come from families of artists. We both carry within us transformational relationships with our mothers. We are dedicated to our Mvskoke culture. Our cultural ways have taught us to respect the processes of living and dying. From this, we have collaborated on a book that is an offering to assist those bearing grief, to help others through to healing in this human journey. We ask that it be done with *vnoketkv* and *vrakkueckv,* with a love for people and ongoing respect for this mysterious and beautiful life.

Mvto.

—Joy Harjo

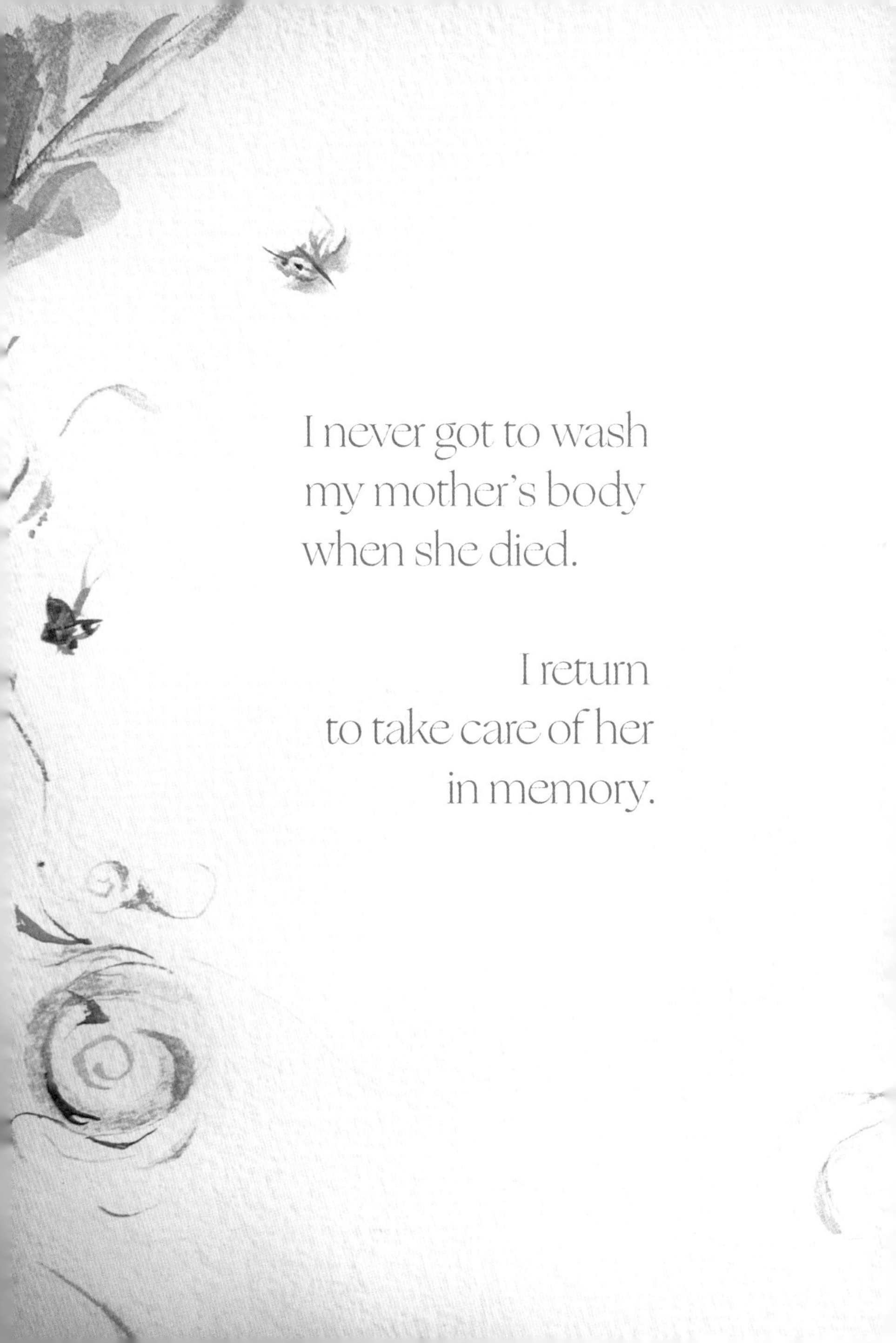

I never got to wash
my mother's body
when she died.

I return
to take care of her
in memory.

That's how I make peace
when things are left undone.

I go back
and open the door.

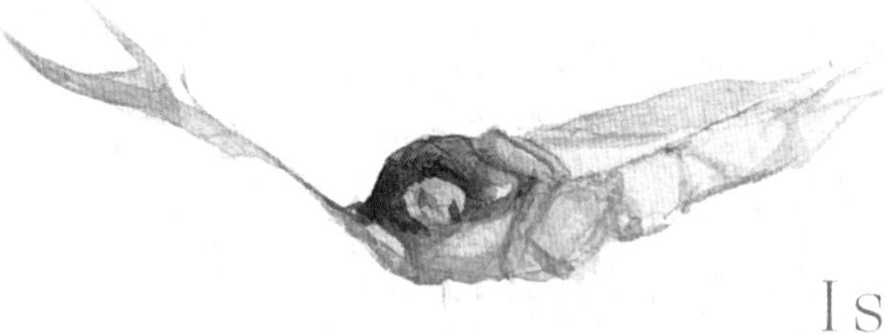

I step in
to make my ritual.
To do what should
have been done,

what needs to be fixed
so that my spirit can move on.

So that the children
and grandchildren
are not caught in a knot

of regret they do not understand.

I find the white enamel pan she used

to bathe us when we were babies.

I turn the faucet on
and hold my hand
under the water

until it is warm,
the temperature one uses
to wash an infant.

I find a clean washcloth
in a stack of washcloths.

She had nothing
in her childhood.

She made sure she had
plenty of everything

when she grew up
and made her own life.

Her closets were full
of pretty dresses,

so many
she had not time
to wear them all.

They were bought
by the young girl
who wore the same
flour sack dress

to school every day,
the one she had to
wash out every night,

and hang up to dry
near the wood stove.

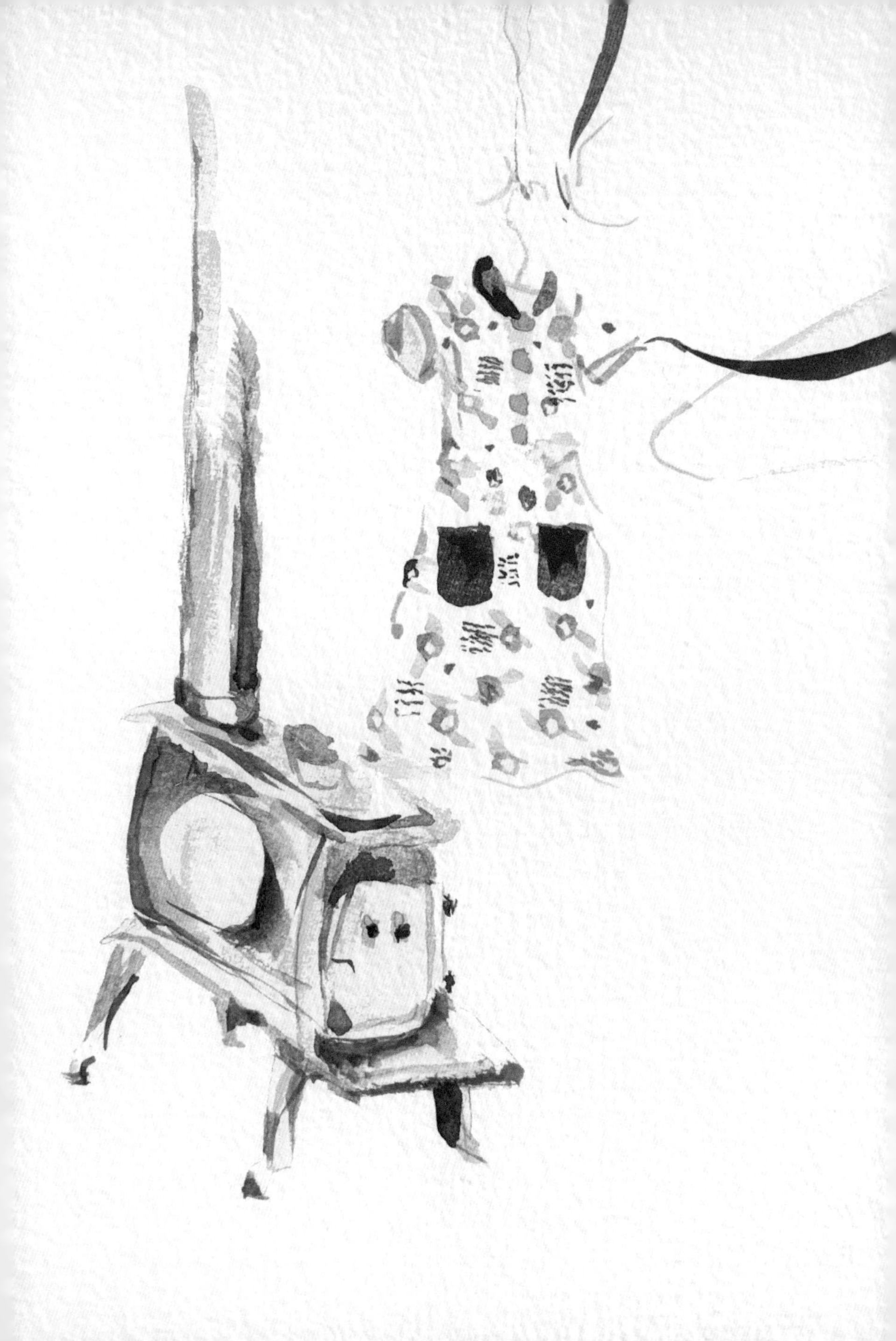

I pick up
the bar of soap
from her sink,

the same soap
she used
yesterday morning
to wash her face.

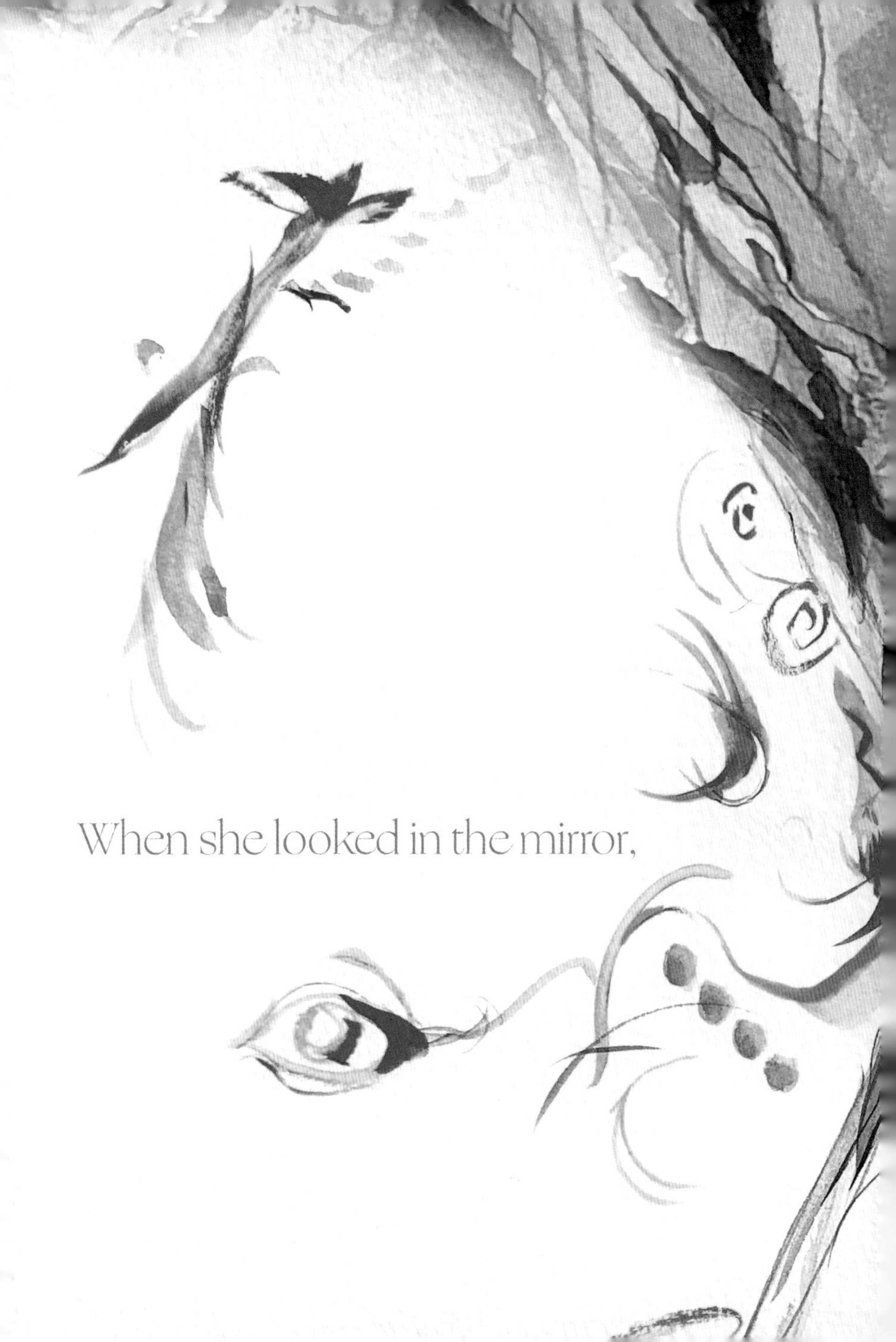

When she looked in the mirror,

did she know it would be
her last sunrise?

I move over pill bottles,
a clock radio on the table
by the bed,

a pen, and set down the pan.
I straighten the blankets over her,

to keep her warm,
for dignity.

I start with her face.
Her face is unlined
even two months before

her eightieth birthday.
She was known
for her beauty.

My mother kept the iron pot
given to her by her mother,

whose mother said
it was given to her
by the U.S. government
on the Trail of Tears.

She grew flowers in it.

As I wash my mother's face,
I tell her

how beautiful she is, how brave,
how her beauty and bravery

live on in her grandchildren.
Her face is relaxed, peaceful.

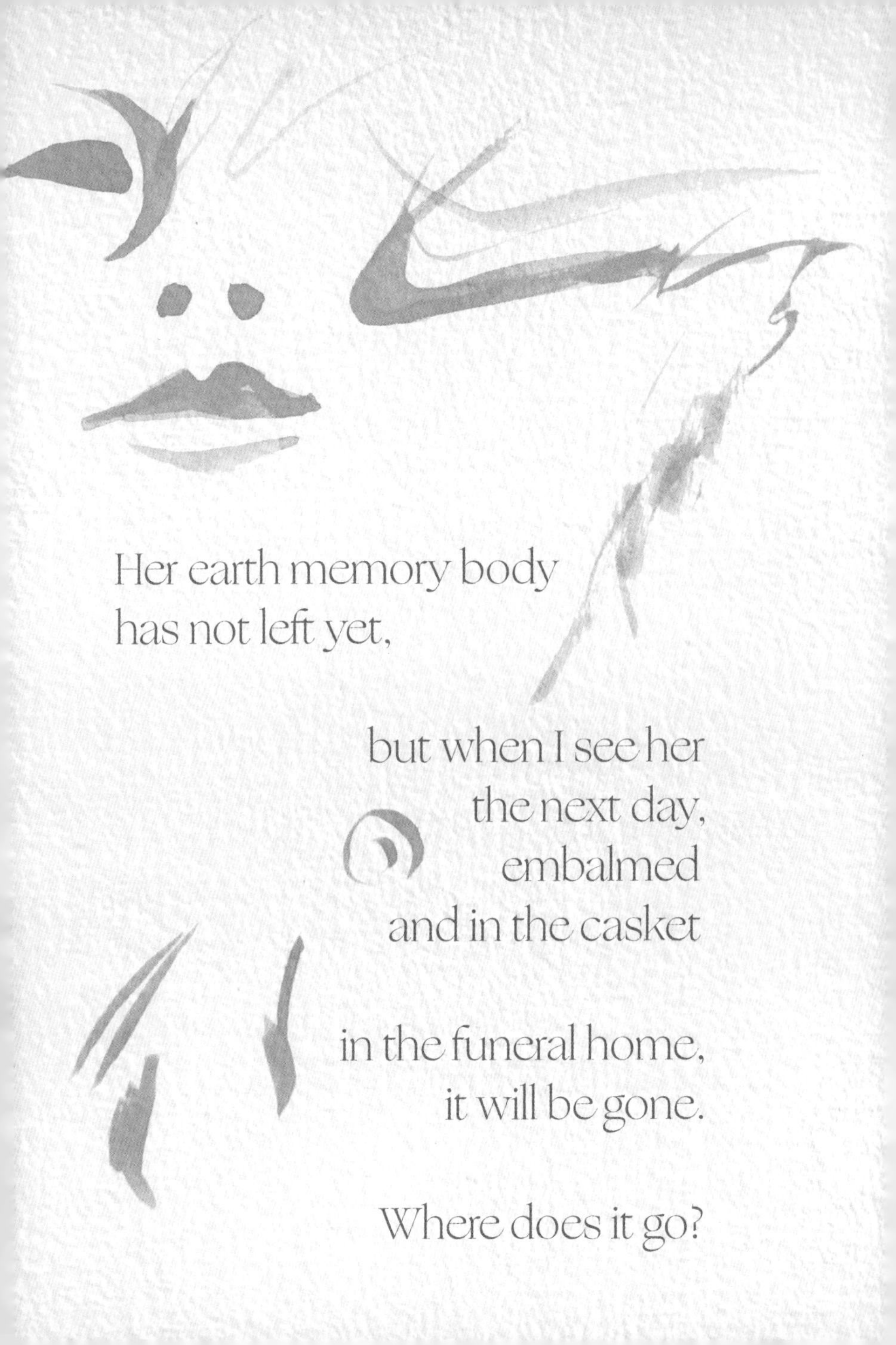

Her earth memory body
has not left yet,

but when I see her
the next day,
embalmed
and in the casket

in the funeral home,
it will be gone.

Where does it go?

It is heavier than the spirit
who lifted up and flew.

I think of it making the rounds
to every place it has loved
to say goodbye.

Goodbye
to the house
where I brought
my babies home,
she sings.

Goodbye to June's Bar where
I was the shuffleboard queen.

I cannot say goodbye yet.

I will never say goodbye.

I lift up each arm to wash.
Her hands still wear
her favorite rings.

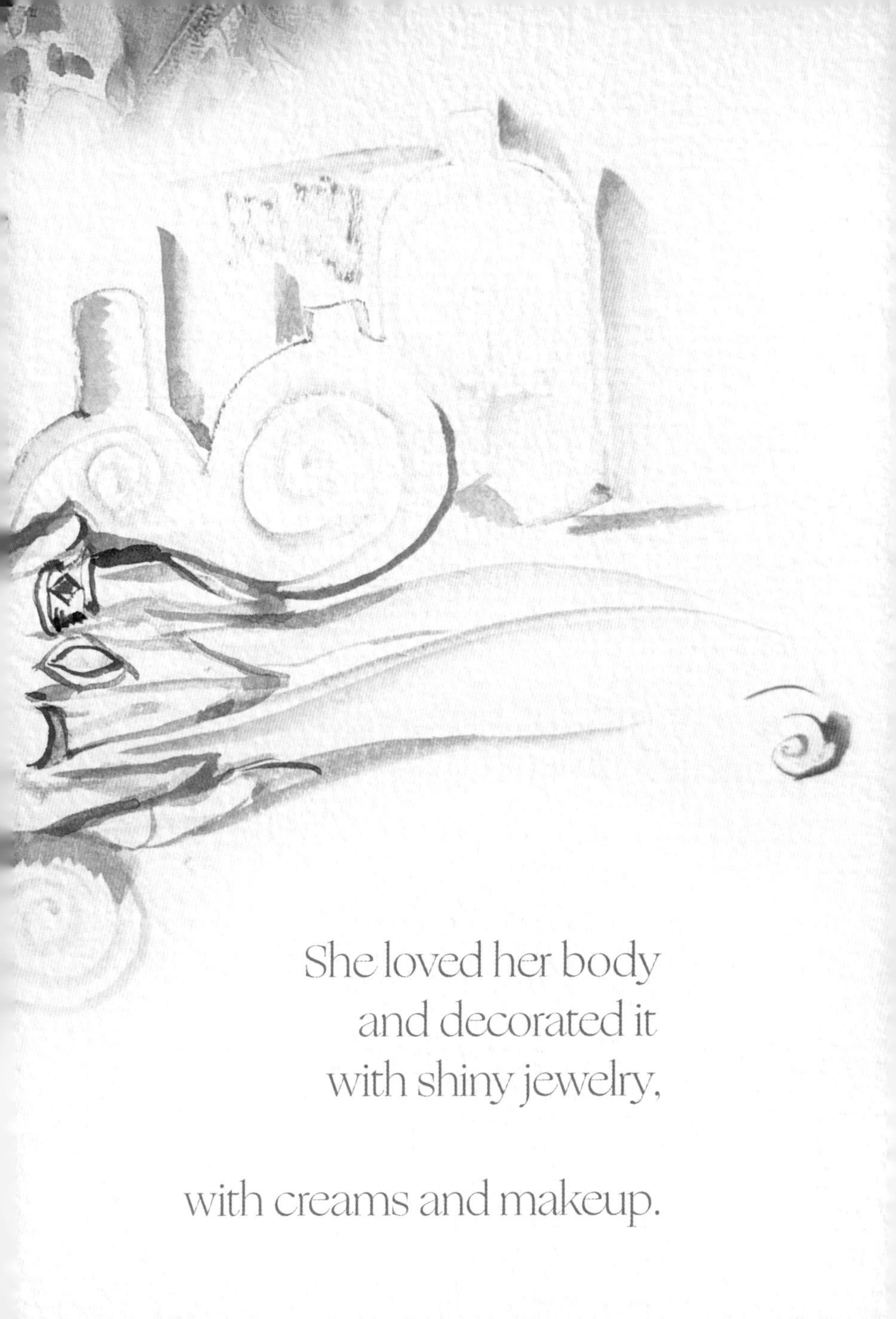

She loved her body
and decorated it
with shiny jewelry,

with creams and makeup.

I am tender
over that burn scar
on her arm

from when she cooked
at the place
with the cruel boss

who insisted she reach
her hand into the Fryolator
to clean it.

She had protested
it was still hot,
and suffered a deep burn.

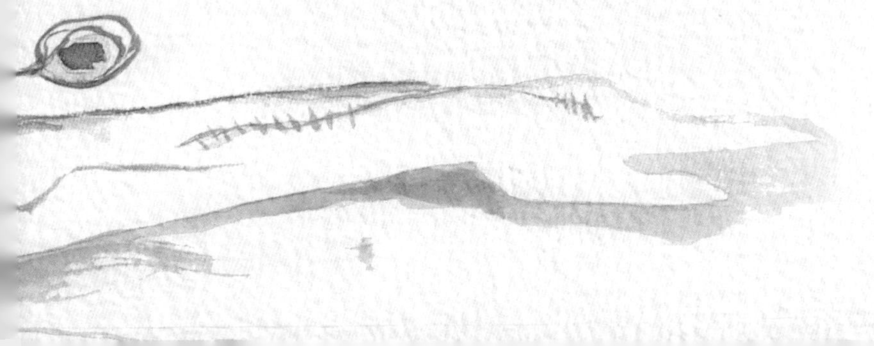

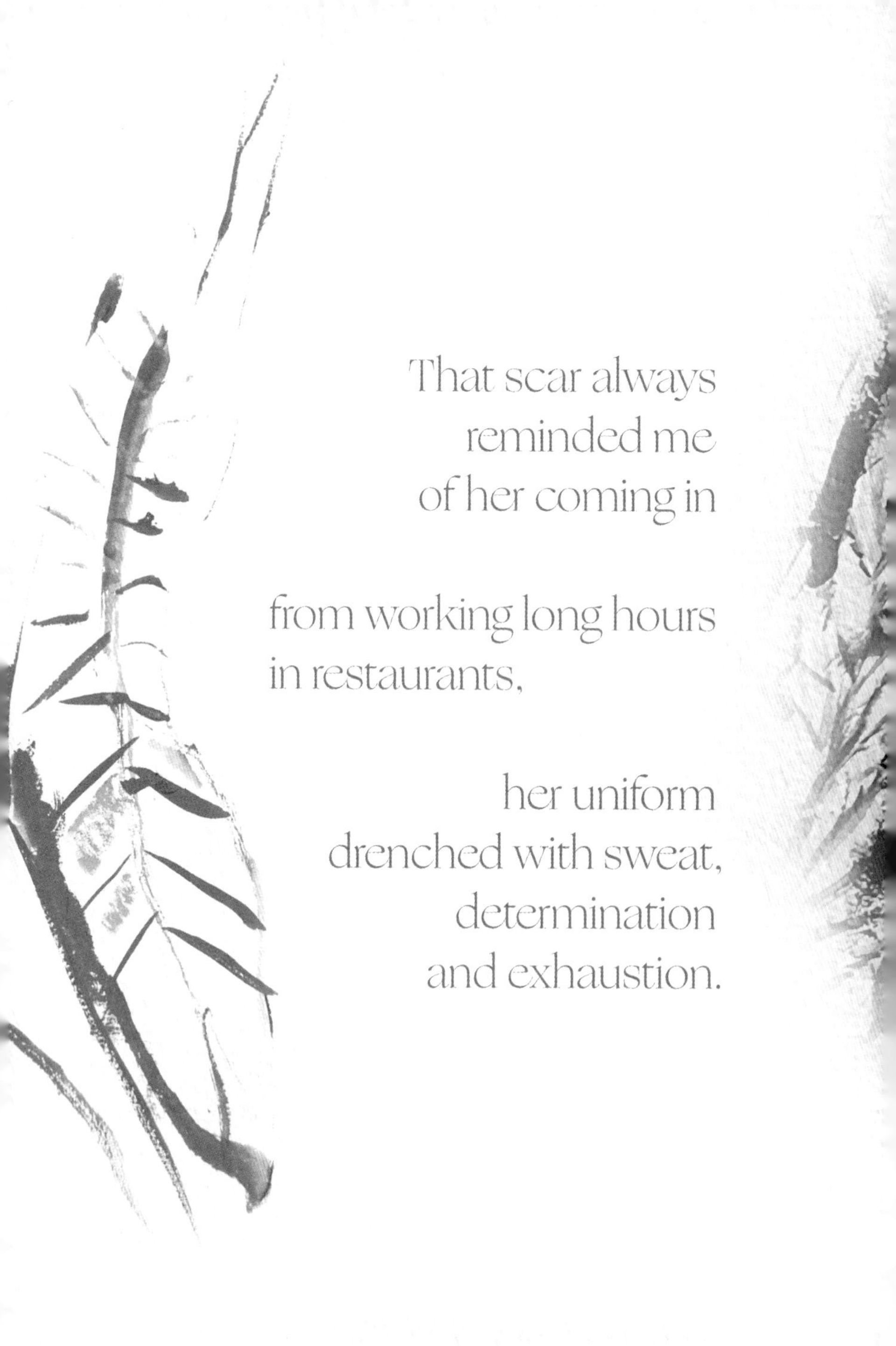

That scar always
reminded me
of her coming in

from working long hours
in restaurants,

her uniform
drenched with sweat,
determination
and exhaustion.

Once she came home
and I was burning up with a fever.

She pulled out the same pan
I am dipping the washcloth in now,

only she's added
rubbing alcohol
to bring the fever down.

She washes tenderly,
tells me about how
her friend Chunkie

left her husband again,
how she knows her old boss,

a Jewish woman
who treated her kindly,

has cancer.
She doesn't know
how she knows;
she just knows.

She doesn't tell me that—

I find it in a journal
she has left me,

a day book in which
she has written notes

for me to find
when she is gone.

I wash her neck,
lift the blankets
to move down
to her heart.

I thank her body
for carrying us
through the tough story,

through the violence
of my father,
and her
second husband.

The story is
all there,
in her body,
as I wash her
to prepare her

to be let down
into earth,
and return all stories
to the earth.

My body memories
rise up as I wash.

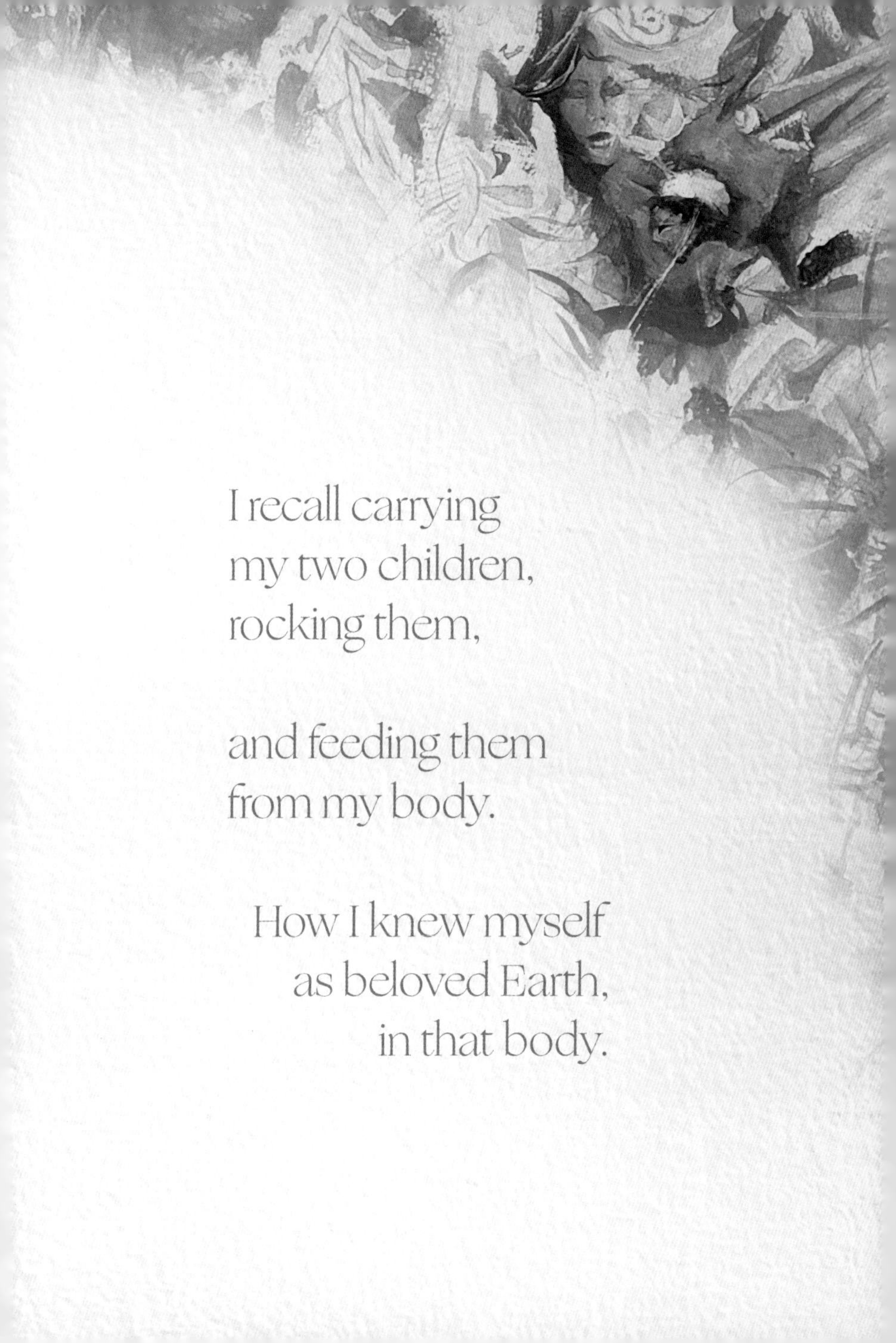

I recall carrying
my two children,
rocking them,

and feeding them
from my body.

How I knew myself
as beloved Earth,
in that body.

I uncover my mother's legs.

I remember
the varicose veins
that swelled like rivers

when my mother
would get off a long shift
of standing and cooking.

They carried more than
a woman should carry.

A woman should be
honored like a queen,

traditionally
we treated our women
with that kind of respect,

my Creek husband
tells me.

Ha, I laugh and ask him,
"then why aren't you
cooking my dinner?"

I wash her feet,
caress them.

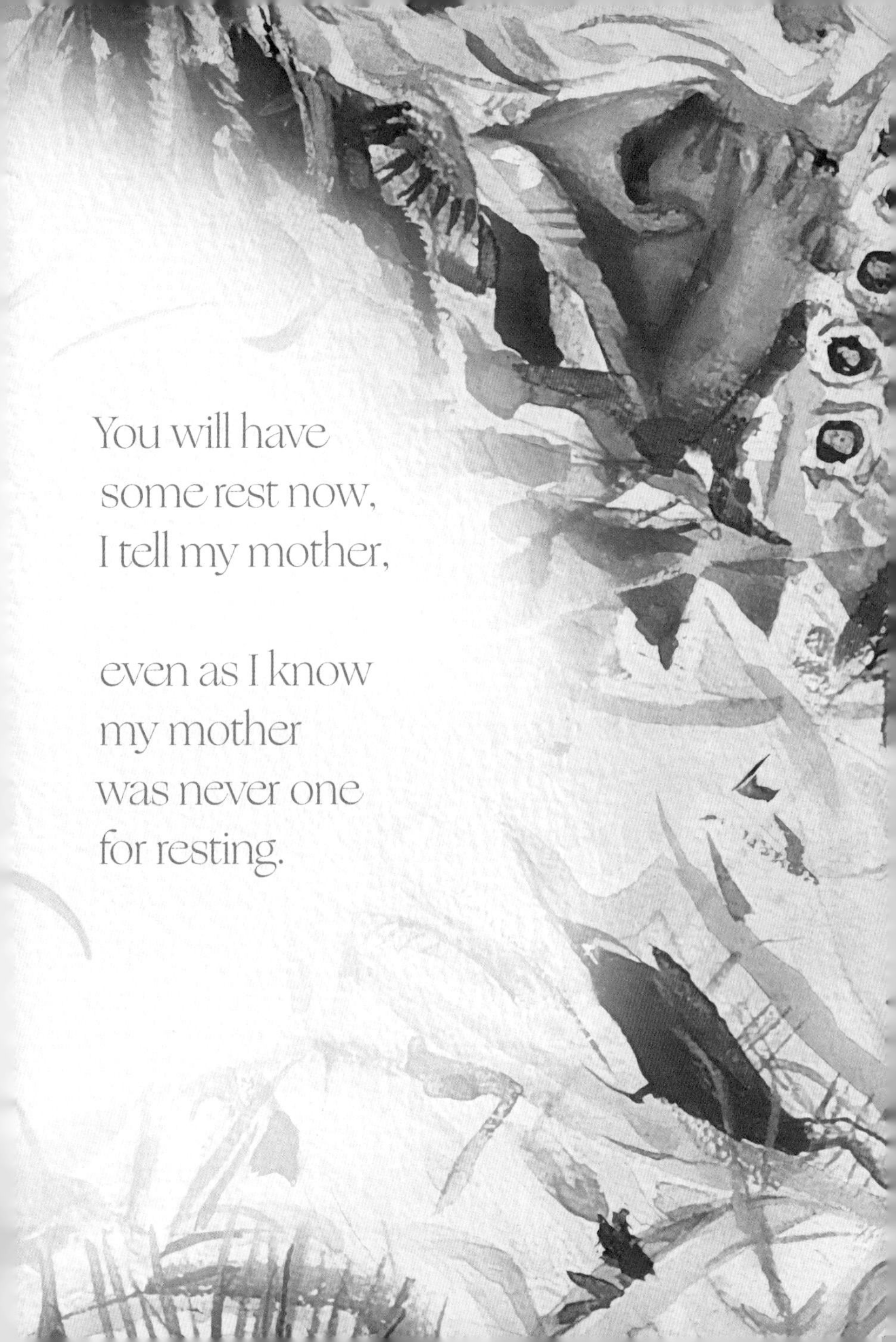

You will have
some rest now,
I tell my mother,

even as I know
my mother
was never one
for resting.

I cover her.

I make the final wring
of the washcloth and
drape it over the pan.

I brush my mother's hair
and kiss her forehead.

I ask the keepers
of the journey
to make sure her travel
is safe and sure.

I ask the angels,
whom she loved
and with whom
she spoke frequently,

to take her home,
but wait,
not before I find
her favorite perfume.

Then I sing
her favorite song, softly.

I don't know
the name of the song,
just a few phrases,

one of those old homemade
heartbreak songs

where there's
a moment of happiness

wound through—

and then I let her go.

Artist's Statement

The first time I remember seeing Joy Harjo was when she was a guest at my college. I was no longer a student but had been asked to do a painting in honor of her visit. I don't remember what was said between us—I just remember how I felt in awe of her presence and the way she spoke.

I've always been in awe of strong women. I was in awe of my mother. When I was a child, I swooned when my mother walked into my classroom and the other kids got to see her.

Somewhere over time, Joy and I became friends. I learned that we were relatives. I learned how to pray and at times I'd call for her strong prayers.

When I was asked if I thought I could fulfill what was needed for this book, I said yes. Parkinson's disease hinders my abilities to think, walk, and create at times, but in May 2023—Joy's birth month and the month my brother Chris was killed at the age of twenty-two—I gathered some items from around the land that surrounds our family art gallery. I made a prayer, asked for help, and began painting the face of a daughter looking down toward her mother the earth.

In my painting, the plants of medicine, prayer, and food float amidst the four directions. The Evening Star shines between two oaks and a hickory that turns into a cedar, leading to the doorway of a circle where we give thanks for the love shared, for all we've been given and survived, and where we pray for the future.

The house my mother built on thirty acres when I was in the fifth grade is filled with the many books she loved, the art created by those who stayed there, and ghosts who never leave. My husband, daughter, grandson, and I take care of it best as we're able. Our son and nephew stay at the gallery in town on Muscogee land that I think of as the center of the universe.

The painting I created for this book, which I've come to call *Most Valuable Power*, has all of that in it. I painted it until February of the next year, the month of my mother's birth and death. I told Joy the painting was too powerful and that I had to stop. My grandson was running around, acting crazy. She said she understood. I thought it would be my last painting.

As I write this, it's the last day of July 2024. I'm in my mother's bed next to her east window. Two nights ago, I woke up and saw something small but extremely bright hovering amidst the trees outside that window. July 29 is my brother's birthday. Eight years ago on that day in this house, Uncle Tony, who helped raise us, passed away in his room next to his bed. Exactly nine months later, my grandson Aiden Jerome was born. He sleeps in the bedroom that was mine when I was growing up. From that room, you can see three trees that grow together on the hill where I sat and watched the sun go down after my mother passed in my arms, with her beloved books, pictures of family, and art all around her.

That evening, the only star in the western sky showed itself brightly and distinctly between the sibling trees. My mother was with me still.

Mvto Joy Harjo. *Mvto* to all who strive and care.

—Dana Tiger

Early stages of *Most Valuable Power*

Most Valuable Power

Acknowledgments

With gratitude for my mother's tough and ever-present spirit. She told me she would be closer to me when she passed. She has been true to her word and is there at every crossroads. My husband, Owen Sapulpa, for standing by me through the many stories of transformation. With gratitude for my grandchildren and their aunt. Together we washed my daughter's, their mother's, and their aunt's body as an act of respect and love for her story and how it will continue to live within us. Gratitude for the perfect team at Ten Speed Press: Kaitlin Ketchum, editorial director; Kelly Booth, creative director; and Kausaur Fahimuddin, editorial assistant. And always with gratitude for Jill Bialosky, my editor for the poem, and Jin Auh and the Wylie Agency for taking care of details past, present, and future. Gratitude to Jennifer Foerster for her assistance in all things literary that come across my desk, and Kathy Anderson who assisted in making this book happen. And *mvto* especially for Dana Tiger, who has inspired me from the beginning, and to her mother for the gift of Dana in this story field.

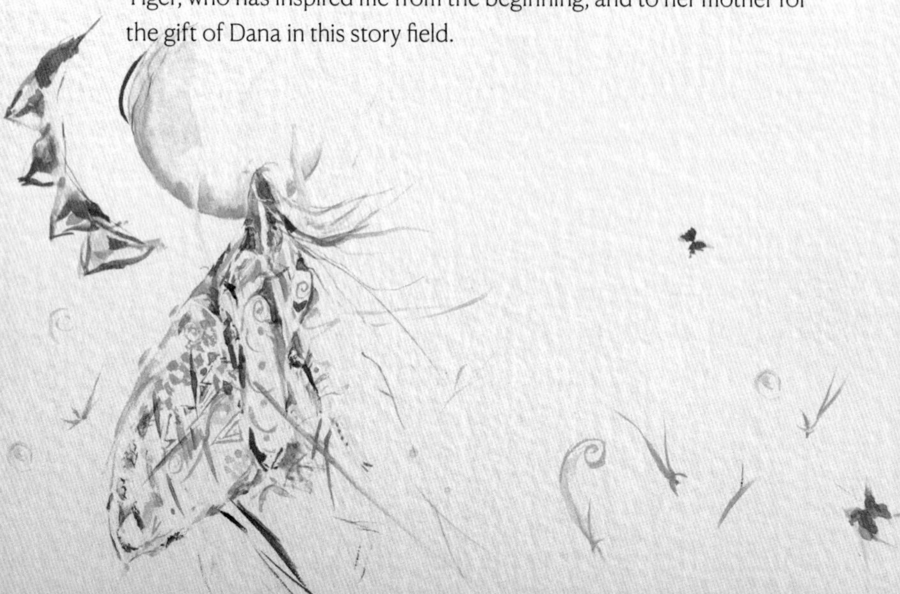

About the Author

JOY HARJO served three terms as the twenty-third Poet Laureate of the United States from 2019 to 2022. She is the author of several poetry collections, plays, children's books, and memoirs, as well as the editor of multiple anthologies of Native poetry. She has also produced several recordings of original music. Harjo has been honored with the Poetry Society of America's Frost Medal, Yale University's 2023 Bollingen Prize for American Poetry, and the National Book Critics Circle's Ivan Sandrof Life Achievement Award, among many other accolades. She also holds honorary doctorates from multiple universities, including Harvard University, the University of St Andrews, and the Institute of American Indian Arts. She is the first artist-in-residence at the Bob Dylan Center in Tulsa, Oklahoma. She is a Muscogee Nation–enrolled citizen and lives in the Muscogee (Creek) Nation reservation in Oklahoma.

About the Artist

DANA TIGER is an award-winning, internationally acclaimed artist. She is a member of the Muscogee (Creek) Nation and is of Seminole and Cherokee descent. Tiger is best known for her watercolors and acrylic paintings depicting the strength and determination of Native American women. Tiger is an inductee into the Oklahoma Women's Hall of Fame and is the founder of Legacy Cultural Learning Community, a nonprofit that nurtures creativity in young Native Americans.

Published in the United States by Ten Speed Press, an imprint of the Crown Publishing Group, a division of Penguin Random House LLC, New York.
TenSpeed.com

TEN SPEED PRESS and the Ten Speed Press colophon are registered trademarks of Penguin Random House LLC.

Typefaces: Sharp Type's Ogg and Commercial Type's Canela

Library of Congress Cataloging-in-Publication Data is on file with the publisher. Library of Congress Control Number: 2024947

Hardcover ISBN: 978-1-9848-6136-8
eBook ISBN: 978-1-9848-6137-5

Printed in China

Editor: Kaitlin Ketchum
Production editor: Sohayla Farman | Editorial assistant: Kausaur Fahimuddin
Art director and designer: Kelly Booth | Production designer: Mari Gill
Production manager: Jane Chinn
Copyeditor: Mi Ae Lipe | Proofreader: Kate Bolen
Publicist: Felix Cruz | Marketer: Monica Stanton

10 9 8 7 6 5 4 3 2 1

First Illustrated Edition